Ghana Cookbook

FAST, EASY, AND AUTHENTIC GHANAIAN RECIPES FOR BEGINNERS

Selassie Boakye

Copyright © 2022 by Selassie Boakye

All rights reserved worldwide.

Without the publisher's express consent, no portion of this book may be duplicated or communicated in any way, whether it be electronically or mechanically, including by photocopying, recording, or information storing and retrieval systems.

Warning-Disclaimer

This Ghanaian Cookbook aims to give people ideas about Ghanaian recipes. We cannot guarantee that everyone will be successful by following the book.

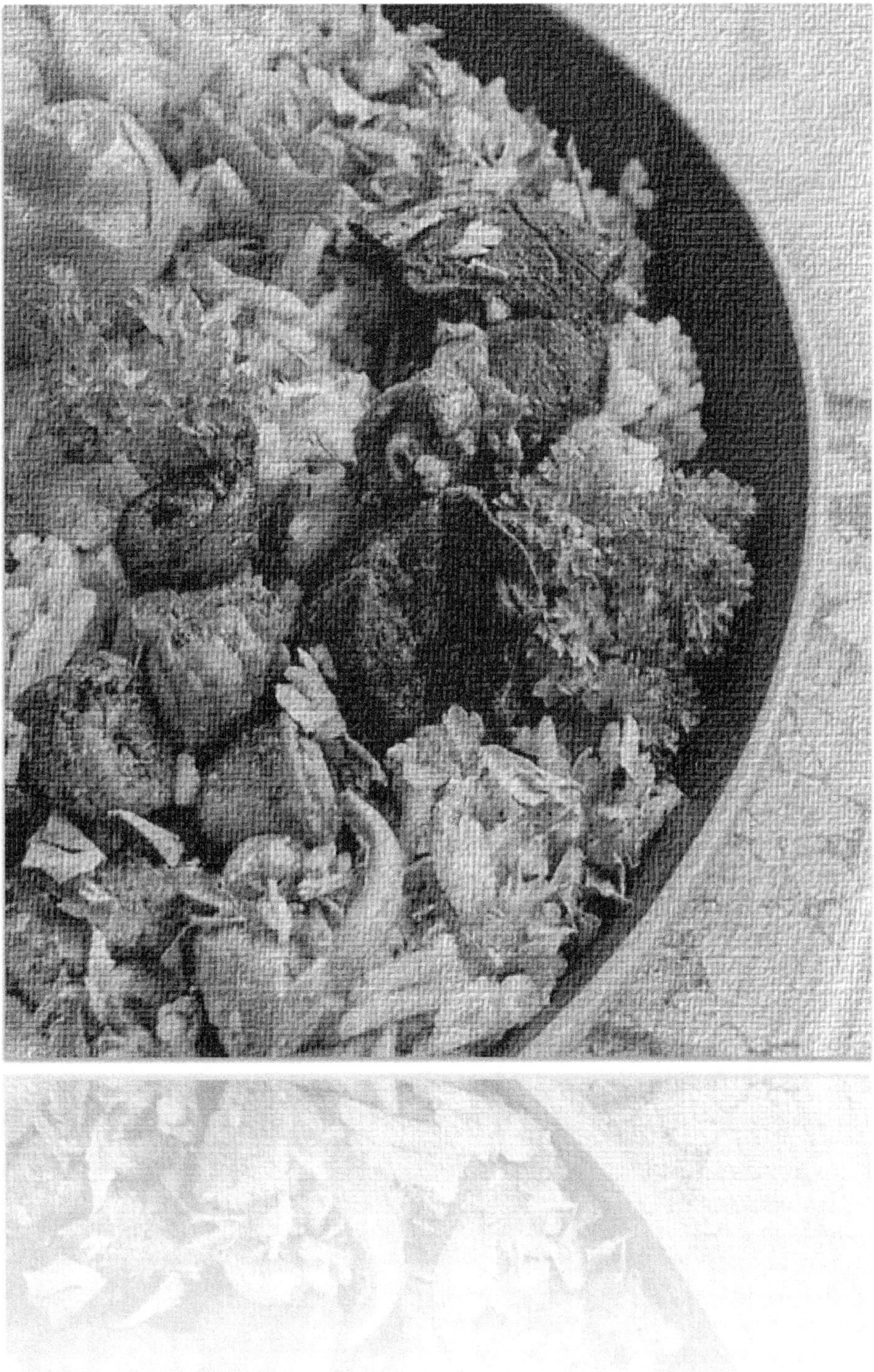

Contents

CHAPTER -1
INTRODUCTION 6
    HISTORY AND FOOD 6
    IMPORTANT INGREDIENTS...9
    WHAT DO GHANAIANS EAT DURING THE DAY?.......................................13
    MEALS FOR HOLIDAYS AND RELIGIOUS CELEBRATIONS 17

BREAKFAST..19
    HAUSA KOKO RECIPE...19
    GHANAIAN WAAKYE 20
    TUO ZAAFI 21
    BANKU...22
    GHANAIAN RED RED STEW 23
    RICE WATER 24
    GARI FOTOR WITH SARDINES 25

ACCOMPANIMENTS..26
    FRIED YAM 26
    RICE BALLS...27
    BANKU...28
    WAAKYE (RICE AND BEANS) 29
    TZ (TUO ZAAFI)..30

DRINKS 31
    SOBOLO DRINK (ROSELLE CALYX DRINK) 31
    TAMARIND DRINK 32

ONE-POT DISHES 33
    DAWADAWA JOLLOF WITH GUINEA FOWL 33
    TOMATO SAUCE FOR TUBAANI 34
    SPAGHETTI (PASTA) JOLLOF 35

TUBAANI (STEAMED COWPEA PUDDING) 36
YAM POTTAGE 37

SNACKS 38

SPICED SORGHUM DOUGH PORRIDGE 38
SPICED MILLET FLOUR PORRIDGE 38
ROASTED GROUNDNUTS 39
CORN DOUGH FLOUR PORRIDGE 40
SPICED CORN DOUGH PORRIDGE 40
KOOSE (FRIED COWPEA BEAN CAKE) 41

MAIN DISHES 42

FISH BRA LEAVES SOUP. 42
FISH GROUNDNUT SOUP 44
SHITO 45
FISH OKRA SOUP(DRY) 46
FISH OKRA SOUP(FRESH) 47
FISH BAOBAB (DRY) LEAVES SOUP 48
FISH OKRA STEW 49
FISH JUTE MALLOW LEAVES SOUP. 50
AMARANTH LEAVES STEW 51

SOME AUTHENTIC GHANAIAN RECIPES 52

SPINACH STEW 52
BEEF STEW 53
PALM-NUT SOUP 54
NEW WAAKYE RECIPE 55
PEANUT BUTTER SOUP 56
CHICKEN STEW 57
GRILLED TILAPIA 58
MEAT PIE 59
SALMON SOUP 61
RICE BALLS 62
KOOSE BLACK EYED-BEAN FRITTERS 63
BAKED PLANTAINS 64
PURE JOLLOF RICE 64
LIGHT SOUP 66
BOFROT 67

RECIPES INFORMATION 68

CONCLUSION 69

Chapter-1

INTRODUCTION

Ghanaian cuisine is a fusion of traditional African flavors and influences from worldwide, including Europe and Asia. Ghanaian cuisine consists primarily of hot soups and stews prepared with tomatoes, onions, pepper, ginger, and other locally grown spices. Stews are thick and frequently served with starchy tubers like plantains or the West African yam. Light soups are filled with starchy sides from tubers, including maize, cassava, cocoyam, and West African yam. If not eating rice, we usually eat a starchy or swallowed tuber. The varieties include plain rice, jollof rice, waakye, agwa mu, and fried rice.

HISTORY AND FOOD

The first people of Ghana lived there as early as 6000 B.C. Early hunter-gatherer communities, most of which resided near the ocean, may have existed, as evidenced by the discovery of ancient stone tools and other artifacts. These nomadic tribes (those that moved about) wandered the countryside for fruit, wild seeds, and animal herds to hunt for meals.

There were ancient trading networks before the first European settlers arrived in 1471. Throughout the African continent, trade routes traveled from north-south and east-west, many of which passed via Ghana. Modern-day Ghana imported salt, dates, tobacco, and copper from the northern areas in exchange for ostrich feathers, cloth, and cola nuts.

The first Europeans to visit present-day Ghana were the Portuguese in 1471. The explorers started fortifying the coastline and bartering with inland tribes for their gold, even though they searched for a sea direction to the Far East. The Dutch and English started exploring Ghana in about 1600. The Germans and Danes erected forts a century later to find ivory and gold. In exchange, explorers sent the tribespeople rum, cotton, textiles, trinkets, and weapons. Later, Ghanaians were forcibly taken prisoner by Europeans and sold as enslaved people.

By the middle of the 1800s, Ghana exported palm oil, pepper, corn, ivory, and gold. All other European powers had been expelled by the British by 1902, and their new British colony was named Gold Coast (later named Ghana in 1957). The government gave cocoa beans to local farmers to promote the expansion of the cocoa industry to maintain Ghana's economic prosperity. The exports of gold and cocoa remained a significant part of Ghana's economy at the start of the twenty-first century. Other successful income crops include coconuts, rice, palm fruit, cola nuts (the main component of many cola beverages), bananas, and numerous citrus fruits.

A LIST OF SOME VEGETABLES/MEALS AND GIVEN THEIR ENGLISH OR SCIENTIFIC NAMES:

- ✓ Exotic Xylopia aethopica (Cloves)
- ✓ Adansonia digitate (Kuuka)
- ✓ Solanum lycopersicum (Tomatoes)
- ✓ Amaranthus cruentus (Aleefu)
- ✓ African locust bean (Dawadawa)
- ✓ Arachis hypogaea (Groundnut)
- ✓ African Xylopia aethopica (Hwenta)
- ✓ Fried cowpea (bean) cake (Koose)
- ✓ Fried groundnut rings (Kulikuli)
- ✓ Corchorus olitorious (Ayoyo)
- ✓ Hibiscus cannabinus (Bra)
- ✓ Steamed cowpea pudding (Tubaani)
- ✓ Tuo Zaafi (TZ)
- ✓ Abelmoschus esculentus (Okra)
- ✓ Tamarindus indica (Puha)
- ✓ Roselle Calyx drink (Sobolo)
- ✓ Rice and Beans (boiled) (Waakye)

IMPORTANT INGREDIENTS

AROMATICS

The holy trifecta includes ginger, onion, and pepper for Ghanaian soups and stews. Every soup and stew must have heat and spice because Ghanaians adore both flavors. They serve as the base for many Ghanaian dishes, along with tomatoes.

LEGUMES

Ghanaian cuisine is plant-friendly because of the vast quantity of legumes we eat. Black-eye peas are the most common among the beans, which are all members of the cowpea family. Black-eye peas come in a variety of shapes and hues. They may be roasted and used for porridge or cooked, steamed, mashed, and fried into kose or tuubani. We also eat groundnut called Bambara beans in addition to cowpeas. These are native to Sub-Saharan Africa and are available in many hues. They pair well with plantains and are pretty nutrient-dense. Additionally, significant amounts of northern-grown soybeans are consumed in Ghana.

GREENS AND VEGETABLES

In forested areas, foods made using cocoyam leaves are prevalent. Many know nkontomire stew, palava sauce made with cocoyam leaves, red palm oil, tomatoes, and agushie. For a fast meal, abomu is cooked and mashed with onions, tomatoes, and pepper in the Ashanti area. Additionally, it is included in ebunu ebunu, a tasty and therapeutic soup. We also consume a variety of greens, the names of which I need to become more familiar with, in addition to cocoyam leaves. Jute mallow, or ademe, is another common green used in soups, particularly in northern Ghana. It is slippery.

We do consume veggies in Ghana, just like everyone else. To mention a few, you will frequently see cabbage, carrots, and green peppers. Garden eggs are a typical local vegetable. These resemble little eggplant in terms of appearance, with yellowish-white skin. Okra is a West African delicacy that is very well-liked. Lastly, many Ghanaians add turkey berries (abedru) to stews and soups. In addition to flavor, they include iron and antioxidants.

GRAINS AND TUBERS

The staple cuisine of Ghana is tubers. We rotate eating a variety of tubers every day. Cassava and cocoyam, crucial components of fufu, were brought to the continent through commerce. But the West African Yam is the king of all tubers. This is the main starch consumed in various stews in Southern Ghana. It is a substitute for french fries at many restaurants and is often boiled or fried. Some people add yam to their fufu.

Grains are adored in Ghana. These are often raised in the north and make up most northern diets. These grains include rice, guinea corn, sorghum, fonio, pearl millet, and sorghum. The grains are either turned into flour or used to produce some of the world's most well-known porridges, including Tom Brown and Hausa Kokoko (spicy millet porridge).

RICE

The two known rice cultivars are Oryza Sativa (from Asia) and Oryza Glaberimma (African). While many African nations now only sell Asian species, the African variety is still crucial to our diet since specific regional specialties call for it. They come in various heights, colors, and forms and, depending on the color, can be prepared similarly to how brown or white rice is.

SEEDS AND NUTS

In Ghana, nuts and seeds constitute a staple of the cuisine. The preferred choice varies depending on where in Ghana a person is. Shea nuts are a staple food in the north. Shea butter makes various foods, including dafaduka, a native Jollof rice dish, and cosmetic goods.

The palm nut and coconut grow more prevalent as you travel south. Numerous soups and stews made in Ghana must contain red palm nuts. They are native to West Africa and typically grow in agroforests with cocoa and cassava plants or the wild. Soups and stews use the entire nut, including the kernel and shaft.

Peanuts are standard in soups, morning cereal, and roadside snacks. You'll probably eat some of the tastiest and freshest peanut butter you've ever had in Ghana. Castor, pepper, and agushie seeds, whole and minced bean, grains, flour, and rice

SPICES

Ghana is unique since we employ a variety of local spices. Some of these spices could be recognizable if you're familiar with Nigerian cuisine. However, I believe that, unlike other West African nations, Ghanaian food uses native herbs far more frequently.

Prekese (Tetrapleura tetraptera), grains of Selim (hwentia), from wisa (alligator pepper), esoro wisa (negro pepper), calabash nutmeg (whediaba), and fermented African locust beans are essential spices (dawa dawa). They are a staple in everything from oatmeal to rice dishes, soups, and stews.

Ghanaians are pretty experimental with spices in addition to their native varieties. Numerous curry powder, anise seeds, nutmeg, cloves, star anise, and coriander seeds are also used in stews, soups, and rice dishes.

WHAT DO GHANAIANS EAT DURING THE DAY?

After discussing the elements, let's examine what Ghanaians consume daily. While we offer certain meals for breakfast and lunch, many of these dishes may also be eaten in the evening. Some breakfast items are also provided in the evening. Certain meals are offered from early morning until midday, depending on what a person seeks. The dishes listed below are favorites. It needs to be a complete list of all the foods consumed in Ghana.

BREAKFAST

People genuinely take eating breakfast quite seriously. Families have diverse diets, but I've emphasized a few traditional foods.

- ❖ Hausa, The breakfast of champions, is Koko. It is a fermented millet porridge with pepper, ginger, calabash nutmeg, cloves, and Selim grains. It has a mild heat, and fresh kose is the ideal accompaniment (Nigerians call this Akara). It is a naturally vegan breakfast that is healthful as long as it isn't overly sweet.

- ❖ Ghanaians prepare a variety of breakfasts at home, along with tea and bread topped with eggs. Either sugar bread, butter bread, or tea bread is available. Covered in a thick layer of margarine (we are less of a butter kind of people and more margarine, which means I, too, can enjoy some)

- ❖ If you're looking for something filling, waakye can be the right option. Waakye in the morning, indeed! It has a perfect combination of carbohydrates, protein, veggies, and toppings. You'll be prepared for the whole day with it!

- Tom Brown, a roasted grain and bean porridge made with roasted black eye peas, roasted millet, roasted maize, roasted peanuts, and spices, is another option for breakfast.

- Less common choices include corn grits and rice water (oblayo)

- vegan egg and sugar bread with Hausa Koko and kosetom brown peanuts

DINNER AND LUNCH

STEW AND STARCH

- Ampesi: Ampesi is a kontomire stew with boiling west African yam and apem (green plantain) (palava sauce). The stew's ingredients include palm oil, spices, agushie, and cocoyam leaves cooked in a hot tomato sauce. For added content, some people add beans, referred to as konto-beans.

- Abomu: If you don't have time, you may prepare a fast sauce called abomu when eaten with boiled yam or plantain. Typically, the pottery is mashed with onion, tomato, pepper, and cooked cocoyam leaves. We mix in peanut butter and drizzle hot red palm oil over onions and spices that have been sautéed. The ideal accompaniment is avocado.

- Red Red is sometimes referred to as fried plantains and beans. An all-time favorite lunch dish is plantain and beans. The beans may be put into a tomato-based stew or cooked and fried with seasonings in hot palm oil. Along with the beans, hot, fried plantains and occasionally gari are served (dried cassava couscous).

SWALLOWS

Simply put, a swallow is a ball of some carbohydrate or tuber served with soup or sauce—several variations in methods, flavors, pairings, and tubers. A wide variety of soups and stews escorts these. These are the most common in Ghana. However, countless regional variations are only recognized throughout some of the nations.

NON FERMENTED SWALLOWS

- Fufu. It is pounded cassava and plantain in Ghana. People start to add West African yam as they go further north. Some fufus also include cocoyam. The most common soups accompanying Fufu are light soup, groundnut/peanut, and palm nut.

- TZ: A traditional dish from the north, tuo zaafi is cooked from cassava and cornmeal. This delicate swallow is typically consumed with thick tomato stew and ayoyo soup (jute mallow soup). Sorghum and millet may also be used to make tuo.

- Face the Wall/Kokonte. Kokonte is a particular kind of swallow. It is formed with dried cassava flour baked into a ball. It frequently comes with a selection of soups.

- **Omutuo:** Rice-filled balls White rice is mashed and then molded into a ball to make rice balls, which are rice-based swallows.

FERMENTED SWALLOWS

The fermented corn swallow, known as "kenkey," is consumed in southern Ghana and even Togo. Gas makes him quite different than Fantes. Both have distinct tastes and preparation methods;

the Ga kenkey is wrapped in a maize husk, while the Fanti kenkey is covered in green leaves. Typically, they come with "pepper"—mashed tomato, onion, and pepper—along with shito.

Southern Ghanaians consume banku, fermented corn, and cassava swallow. Although okra soup is typically served, it may be finished with pepper.

STEWS AND SOUPS

Light soup, groundnut, palm nut, and cocoyam leaf are popular soups with Fufu. Okra soup is typically served with banku. However, individuals frequently combine soups and swallows based on what they have at home. Although soups often start with steaming meat, I make mine with mushrooms, which also works. In Ghana, mushrooms are highly popular, and when they are in season, they are frequently used in soups. Other well-liked regional soups in Northern Ghana include dried okra soup and baboab leaf soup. The types of stews vary significantly across the nation.

Along with the previously mentioned nkontomire stew, other stews include beans and a straightforward tomato stew. Since tomato stew is the foundation for so many Ghanaian meals, learning it means mastering a lot of Ghanaian cuisines. Tomato stew can, however, be eaten on its own.

MEALS FOR HOLIDAYS AND RELIGIOUS CELEBRATIONS

The government does not acknowledge the official national religion of Ghana. This is because Ghanaians practice several different religions. About 60 percent of people observe an indigenous religion that predated Christianity and Islam for hundreds of years, while 15 percent identify as Muslims (followers of the Islamic faith). Animism, a term used to describe such viewpoints, is a concept that all things have spirits that can do good and bad fortes to people who come into contact with them.

Although the Portuguese brought Christianity to Ghana in the 1400s, Christian missionaries were most responsible for its expansion in the 1800s. In present-day Ghana, most Christians reside close to the seaside and participate in Christian festivities.

All Christians celebrate Christmas, including Ghanaians, who celebrate it for up to eight days, as a particular time of year. It's when loved ones and friends get together, and kids get new toys and clothes. Chicken is the most often served food during Christmas dinner. However, goats or sheep may also be made. The main course's popular side dishes include yams and stew or soup. Dessert is frequently served with fresh fruit and sweets. Even though they rarely eat pork or drink alcohol, Muslims enthusiastically observe Islamic festivals (such as Ramadan).

Every year, Ghana has over 100 festivals, many based on animistic beliefs and timed to harvest. Usually, they honor their ancestors. Due to these colorful festivities, Ghanaians experience a sense of spiritual and cultural connectedness. All celebrations, even the solemn ones, entail food, singing, and dancing.

Odwira is one of the most well-known festivities in which the new yam crop is offered to one's ancestors. Every year, tight rules are followed during the week-long event in September or October, depending on the harvest. According to one regulation, new yams can only be consumed once the celebration ends. A large feast honoring the living and the dead is hosted on the fourth day before the festival begins, and dinners are also staged in the middle of numerous towns.

A sample menu of Christmas in Ghana

- Chicken, goat, or sheep
- Chicken stew
- Cooked rice or jollof rice
- Boiled soybeans, yams, or eggplant
- Fufu
- Gari biscuits
- Mangoes, oranges, or pawpaws (papayas)

Every year on March 6, Ghana celebrates Independence Day to commemorate 1957, when Ghana gained independence from Great Britain. The celebrations include fireworks, athletic activities, award shows, and cultural performances. On this auspicious day, many people like eating fufu, a delicacy made from yams or plantains (which are related to bananas). Oto, a yam dish, is offered.

Chapter-2

BREAKFAST

Hausa Koko Recipe

Servings: 2-3
Prep: 5 mins
Cook: 20 mins
Total: 25 mins

Ingredients

- 1/2 cup fermented corn or millet dough
- 1/4 teaspoon hot chili powder
- 1/4 teaspoon ground cloves
- 1/2 teaspoon ground ginger
- 3 cups water divided
- kosher salt

Steps

In a medium pot, add fermented corn or millet dough. To form a smooth paste, crumble the fermented dough with 1 cup of cold water. Place in a pan and cook over high heat while stirring periodically.

Stirring continually, add 2 cups of boiling water to the pot, and carry it to a boil. The mixture may start to lump at this stage. To keep the porridge smooth, whisk any lumps out. Add a dash of chili powder, ground ginger, ground cloves, and salt—ten minutes of simmering at low heat with stirring.

When ready to serve, whisk in the appropriate quantity of sugar.

Ghanaian Waakye

Servings-5- 6
Prep Time 10 Mins
Cook Time 50 Mins
Cooling Time 20 Mins
Total Time 1 Hr 20 Mins

Ingredients

- 2 cups rice
- 1 cup black eye beans
- 6-8 waakye leaves
- Salt

Instructions

Select the grits and stones from the beans. After being cleaned, put the beans in the pressure cooker. Waakye should be washed before adding it to pressure cookers. Load the pot with water until it is at the lowest level.
Close the pressure cooker's valve and wait until it reaches maximum pressure. At most, 15 minutes should be needed for this.

Once it reaches maximum pressure, turn the heat down and let the beans simmer for 10 minutes. Remove from heat and for natural cooling to depressurize. It should take a few minutes until the pot has sufficiently cooled. Open the lid. Put the beans in another pot with the waakye leaves and cooking liquid. Pour the washed rice into the pool as well. If additional water is required to cook the rice, add it thoroughly. Salt the saucepan, then cover it. Let the rice finish cooking. The kind of rice used will determine how long it takes. If you need clarification, see the pack directions.

Waakye should be taken out and served with your favorite side.

Tuo Zaafi

Prep Time: 35 Mins
Cook Time: 2 Hr
Total Time: 2 Hr 35 Mins

Ingredients

- bunch Ayoyo leaves
- 300 g meat (beef)
- 1 cups corn flour
- large tomatoes
- 1 cup Cassava flour
- Saltpeter
- 1 tsp powdered fish
- 1 tsp Dawa Dawa
- 1 tsp powdered pepper
- smoked salmon
- 1 tsp fish seasoning
- medium onion
- 1 tsp powdered okro
- 1 tsp all-purpose spices
- 300 g meat (beef)
- 1 cups corn flour
- large tomatoes
- 1 cup Cassava flour
- Herrings

Instructions
Ayoyo leaves must first be cleaned before being chopped into tiny chunks. Water should be added to a pan; after it begins to boil, add powdered fish, okra, and Dawa Dawa; after 2 minutes of

simmering, add saltpeter and the chopped ayoyo leaves. Wait another two minutes before adding salt and other seasonings. Ayoyo soup is now prepared.

The meat must now be prepared. The heart should be cleaned and cut before being placed in a pan over medium heat. Onion and garlic can be chopped or blended, then added to the meat. Season it, then let it cook. After adding the salmon and herrings, add the seasonings and simmer for 10 minutes. Salt to taste should be added last.

We must get maize flour for the tuo zaafi and combine it thoroughly with cold water. The corn flour mixture should be added to boiling water and cooked for 10 minutes. Get some of the corn flour mixes from a different boil and place them aside. Combine some dry corn and cassava dough, add the combination to the cooking corn dough, and stir thoroughly. The corn dough mixture should then be added to the tuo zaafi. For 15 minutes, stir. Soup and stew can then be served alongside your tuo zaafi.

Banku

Servings: 4 people
Prep Time-10 mins
Cook Time-20 mins
Total Time-30 mins.

Ingredients

- ¼ lb cassava dough
- 1 lb corn dough
- One teaspoon salt
- 1 cup water

Instructions

The maize and cassava dough should be smooth after being combined with water; place over high heat and stir regularly.

Depending on how wet the processed dough was initially, more water may be added to make the dough solid but not overly complicated.

Reduce the heat to medium, add one or two tablespoons of water to the saucepan, and let the banku steam for a few minutes. It should take five minutes. After one last stir, turn off the heat and remove the banku. Scoop the necessary quantity into a water basin, then stir until balls form.

Banku can be paired with grilled tilapia, shito, fante fante, or okra stew.

Ghanaian Red Red Stew

Servings: 4 people
Prep Time-20 mins
Cook Time-1 hr 35 mins

Ingredients

- 1/4 cup palm oil
- One onion
- 1 1/2 cup cowpeas
- One teaspoon of curry powder
- 4 to 6 plum tomatoes
- 1 Scotch bonnet
- 1 cup tomato puree
- One tablespoon of tomato paste
- 1/4 pound smoked pork
- 1-inch piece of ginger
- 1 to 3 teaspoons of cayenne
- Salt and black pepper

Instructions

Cowpeas should be cooked until soft in simple water. Salt the pot generously, then cover it and turn off the heat. Set aside at this time.

Heat the palm oil in a medium saucepan over a medium flame. Add the Scotch bonnet and chopped smoked pork when heated, and sauté the onions for approximately 3 minutes. Cook for another two to three minutes. Add the chopped fresh tomatoes after incorporating the cayenne and curry powder.

Cowpeas and the rest of the ingredients should be added. Using a slotted spoon, remove the cowpeas from their water. If some cooking water spills into the pot, that's okay—thirty minutes of simmering after thorough mixing.

Serve with plain white rice or fried plantains.

Rice Water

Prep Time-15 mins
Cook Time-20 mins
Total Time-35 mins.

Ingredients

- 1 cup rice
- 5 cups water
- 1 pinch nutmeg
- Salt
- Sugar
- Evaporated milk
- Hot water

Instructions

Drain the rice after washing it until the water is clear. Five cups of water should be added to the rice bowl.

For around 15 minutes, cook the rice until it is soft. If extra water is required, do so to produce smooth, sticky rice. Put a dash of salt in.

Rice should be crushed using the flat side of a wooden spoon until it becomes mushy and forms a ball. To soften it to the required thickness and consistency, add boiling water.

With a dash of nutmeg, evaporated milk, sugar (or honey), roasted almonds, coconut flakes, or other seasonings, serve the hot rice water.

Gari Fotor With Sardines

Servings-3-4
Prep Time 10 Mins
Cook Time-20 Mins
Cooling Time-15 Mins
Total Time-45 mins.

Ingredients

- 1 ½ cups Garri
- Three tablespoons Palm oil
- 2 Onions sliced
- 2 Garlic chopped
- One teaspoon of Pepper flakes/powder
- ½ cup Stock
- One can Sardine
- ½ teaspoon Ginger powder
- One teaspoon of Mild curry powder
- Two tablespoons of Tomato puree
- Two handfuls of chopped spinach
- Salt
- 2 Tomatoes chopped for garnish

Instructions

Remove the sardines from the can and chop them up. To make a paste, combine the tomato puree and pepper flakes in a small bowl with two tablespoons of water. The onions are added to the hot oil in the pan. The onions are in hot oil until transparent. Ginger, curry powder, and garlic are added. Before including the tomato puree and pepper paste, let the mixture simmer for around 30 seconds. Add the pieces of sardine and the stock. Add salt to taste, cover the pan, and simmer for approximately 15 minutes. After releasing from the heat, mix in the spinach. Let it cool. Add water to the garri to make it wet while the sauce cools. Add just enough water to moisten it without making it mushy. Mix well after adding the sauce to the wet garri.

Serve alongside the diced tomatoes.

ACCOMPANIMENTS

Fried yam

Ingredients

- Two teaspoons of salt
- 850 g sliced yam
- 1500 ml water

Preparation

- ✓ Wash, peel, and cut yam into eatable pieces
- ✓ Wash peeled yam (again)
- ✓ Add washed yam pieces to salt water (2 tablespoons of salt in
- ✓ 1500 ml of water) and allow standing for three minutes

Cooking

Heating oil Sliced yam is deep-fried. Cooking and prevent scorching; turn occasionally. Until done and crispy, fry the yam.

Serve hot with spicy pepper sauce, a little frying oil, and seasoned groundnut powder.

Rice balls

Ingredients

- 800 g rice
- 3000 ml water

Preparation

- ✓ Pick foreign materials from rice and wash them.

Cooking

Boiled water is ready. Stir in the rice and cover. Rice should be very soft after cooking, with additional water added in modest amounts. Rice grains should be broken by vigorous stirring. Combine, then form into balls.

Add groundnut soup to the dish.

Banku

Ingredients

- 1300 g corn dough
- Two tablespoons of salt
- 1000 g cassava dough
- 4000 ml water

Preparation

- ✓ Mash corn and cassava dough together with water
- ✓ Add salt to taste

Cooking

Light the mixture on fire and carefully stir it until it thickens. To transform lumps into a smooth paste, start firmly. If the compound is too dry, add water, cover it, and let it boil for a few minutes. Stir the meal occasionally until it's cooked and the desired texture is achieved. Form into balls, then plate.

Serve with aleefu stew, okra soup, or groundnut soup.

Waakye (rice and beans)

Ingredients

- 500 g cowpeas
- 50 g sorghum leaf stalk
- 1000 g rice
- 4000 ml water
- Salt to taste

Preparation

- ✓ Pick foreign materials from the cowpea and wash
- ✓ Pick foreign materials from rice and rinse to remove stones
- ✓ and dirt
- ✓ Wash sorghum leaf stalk

Cooking

Boiled water is ready. Saltpeter and the stalk of sorghum are added. Stir in the cowpea. Add rice and toss to combine after allowing to boil until cowpeas are halfway cooked. Stir in salt to taste. Let the mixture boil until it is done.

Serve warm.

TZ (Tuo Zaafi)

Ingredients

- 500 g corn flour (whole meal)
- 4250 ml water
- 150 g cassava flour

For dehusked meal

- 450 g corn flour (dehusked)
- 3500 ml water
- 300 g cassava flour

Preparation

- ✓ Mix 1/3 corn flour with enough water
- ✓ Mix remaining corn flour with cassava flour

Cooking

Light a fire to boil some water. Stir in the flour (corn) and water mixture after adding it. To create porridge, cover and bring to a boil while stirring periodically. If it's too thick, add additional water. Get a third of the porridge and set it aside. Sprinkle portions of the corn/cassava flour mixture into the hot porridge.
To prevent the creation of lumps, stir briskly.

Add the reserved porridge a bit if it becomes too thick.
When done, stir (work) against the pot to break up clumps.

Serve with groundnut soup, bra, baobab, ayoyo leaves, okra, or bra.

DRINKS

Sobolo Drink (Roselle Calyx Drink)

Ingredients

- 100 g roselle calyces
- 40 g fresh ginger
- 5 g cloves
- 300 g sugar
- 5 g hwentia
- 4400 ml water

Preparation

- ✓ Pick foreign items from the sorrel leaves
- ✓ Wash and scrape ginger
- ✓ Grind spices – ginger, hwentia, and cloves

Cooking

Roselle calyx is cooked in a spice mixture. Roselle calyces are covered with boiling water, then let stand for 45 minutes. Add the ground spices and mix thoroughly. Until color is removed, cover the container and let it stand.
Set mixture aside to cool.
Filter the liquid and add sugar to taste (common sweeteners – sugar, honey, or fruit juice).
Include flavoring (optional).

Serve cold.

Tamarind Drink

Ingredients

- 200 g tamarind seed
- 2500 ml water
- 80 g ginger
- 3 g alligator pepper
- 5 g cloves
- Sugar to taste

Preparation

- ✓ Scrape and wash ginger.
- ✓ Wash and grind all spices.

Steps

Pouring boiling water over tamarind. Soak for several hours (or overnight). To get the pulp off the seeds, mash the combination. Including ground spices, Add 3000 ml additional water, then boil the mixture for 30 minutes. Place out the fire and let it cool. Remove particles with a sieve and a sieve (spices and pulp).

Serve cold and sweeten to taste.

ONE-POT DISHES

Dawadawa Jollof with Guinea Fowl

Ingredients

- 600 g local rice
- 50 g Dawa Dawa
- 50 g tomato paste
- 20 g fresh hot pepper
- 20 g ground ginger
- 120 g fresh onion
- 320 g fresh tomato
- 500 ml vegetable oil
- 1500 ml water

Preparation

- ✓ Slice onion
- ✓ Grind tomatoes, hot pepper, and ginger

- ✓ Remove stones and foreign materials from rice and wash
- ✓ Pound or crush Dawa Dawa

Cooking

Heat oil by setting it aflame. Include the onion in the heated oil and let it cook or become light brown. Include chopped vegetables (tomato, ginger, hot pepper, and onion). Stir in tomato paste and Dawa Dawa that has been pounded or crushed. Cook in a simmering pot. To taste, add salt and water. Permit to boil. Stir in the rice and leave it to boil until done.

With fried guinea chicken, serve hot.

Tomato sauce for Tubaani

Ingredients

- 280 ml oil
- 140 g onions
- 200 g tomatoes
- 20 g ginger
- 10 g bouillon tablet
- 500 ml of water
- 50 g tomato paste
- 20 g hot pepper
- 50 g powdered fish
- Salt to taste

Preparation

- ✓ Chop onion
- ✓ Grind tomatoes, hot pepper, and ginger

- ✓ Pound dry fish

Cooking

Heating oil Add the onion slices and let them saute. Tomato paste and crushed vegetables are added. Stir in salt to taste before allowing to simmer. Include fish powder after crushing the bouillon tablet. Until the food is done, simmer covered.
accompany with Tubaani.

Spaghetti (pasta) jollof

Ingredients

- 100 ml oil
- 350 g spaghetti
- 200 g tomatoes
- 50 g powdered fish
- 15 g hot pepper
- 10 g bouillon tablet
- 1000 ml water
- 25 g Dawa Dawa
- 150 g onions
- Salt to taste

Preparation

- ✓ Grind vegetables together
- ✓ Pound or crush Dawa Dawa
- ✓ Break spaghetti into desirable pieces
- ✓ Chop onion
- ✓ Pound dry fish

Cooking

Heating oil Add tomatoes, onions, and Dawa Dawa that have been crushed. Include enough water in the pan to cover it, then let it simmer. Add the spaghetti that has been broken. To keep from sticking together, stir. Place a cover on it and cook. Stir periodically with a wooden spoon until soft and all liquid is absorbed.

Serve warm.

Tubaani (steamed cowpea pudding)

Ingredients

- 800 g cowpea flour
- 6500 ml of water

Preparation
Cowpea flour and water should be combined, then beaten in a circular motion until fluffy. Wrap a little of the mixture in each washed leaf (people typically use Thaumatococcus daniellii leaf, banana leaf, or corn husk). On a separate fire, boil water.

Cooking
Place (enough) water on the fire, then adds cover. The saucepan should have a base of part of the (empty) leaves and a top layer of leaves to cover the water. Place the wrapped mixture on the leaves, cover, and steam in the boiling water for about two hours. Pour boiling water over the sides of the pan now and then to avoid

scorching. Steam on until the food is done. Slice, unwrap and extinguish flames.

Hot tomato sauce, spicy groundnut powder, and vegetable oil are recommended (200 ml oil fried with 50 g onion and half a teaspoon powdered hot pepper).

Yam pottage

Ingredients

- 730 g yam
- 120 g fresh onion
- 17 g hot pepper
- 10 g bouillon tablet
- 30 g tomato paste
- 160 g fresh tomatoes
- 200 ml palm oil
- 50 g fish powder
- 1050 ml water
- Salt to taste

Preparation

- ✓ Wash and peel yam and cut it into cubes
- ✓ Grind tomato, onion, and hot pepper
- ✓ Pound dry fish

Cooking

Cubed yams should be placed in a pot with water. Boil by putting it on fire. Add salt, tomato paste, fish powder, and chopped vegetables. Till the yam is tender, let it simmer. Press it on the saucepan with a spoon to thicken the yam. Include palm oil. Allow boiling after adding chopped onion and continuing to cook.

When cooked, then serve.

SNACKS

Spiced sorghum dough porridge

Ingredients

- 200 g spiced sorghum dough
- 2400 ml water

Preparation

- ✓ Mix spiced sorghum dough with enough water and sieve.

Cooking

Light a fire to boil some water. To prevent the creation of lumps, stir the sieved mixture into the boiling water.

Serve it hot after letting it boil until it is done.

Spiced millet flour porridge

Ingredients

- 200 g spiced millet flour
- 1600 ml water

Preparation

- ✓ Spiced millet flour should be combined with enough water to make a dough. The dough should then be allowed to ferment.

Cooking

Light a fire to boil some water. To prevent the creation of lumps, vigorously mix the sieved mixture into the boiling water.

Serve it hot after letting it boil until it is done.

Roasted groundnuts

Ingredients

- 300 g groundnuts
- 550 ml of water
- Two tablespoons salt
- Sea/river sand

Preparation

- ✓ Sort fresh groundnuts and remove foreign materials,
- ✓ stones or dirt
- ✓ Sort to have even sizes

- ✓ Sieve and wash sand to clean the sand

Cooking

Add salt and enough water to a saucepan. Place a lid on it and let it boil. Groundnuts should be added and given two minutes to cook. Drain the water. Spread out and allow to dry in the sun. With river sand, warm a pot (ensure the sand is hot enough). Add the dry nuts, then mix (to roast). To keep the groundnuts from burning, stir them occasionally over low heat. Examine a groundnut seed for doneness by peeling and tasting it.

When the groundnuts are cooked and have a light brown color, remove them from the heat. Shake to remove sand from the roasted groundnuts before pouring them into a metal colander or cane basket. Disperse to cool.

Serve alongside fried or roasted maize, millet, or sorghum porridge.
Made of corn, millet, sorghum, or on its own as a snack.

Corn dough flour porridge

Ingredients

- 200 g corn dough flour
- 2600 ml water

Preparation

- ✓ Combine corn dough with enough water and a sieve.

Cooking

Light the fire to boil some water. To prevent the creation of lumps, vigorously whisk the sieved mixture into the boiling water. If extra water is required, add it. Stir and let cook while boiling.

Serve warm.

Spiced corn dough porridge

Ingredients

- 400 g spiced corn dough
- 2600 ml water

Preparation

✓ Combine corn dough with enough water and a sieve.

Cooking

Light a fire to boil some water. To avoid the formation of lumps, vigorously stir the sieved mixture into the boiling water. Let it cook until it's done. Serve hot

Koose (fried cowpea bean cake)

Ingredients

- 450 g cowpea (dehusked) flour
- 270 ml oil
- 15 g fresh or dry, hot pepper
- One tablespoon salt

- 50 g ginger
- 1000 ml water

Preparation

- ✓ Cowpea flour and water should be combined, then beaten circularly until fluffy.
- ✓ Scrape the ginger
- ✓ Cleanse and crush the onion, ginger, and hot pepper.
- ✓ Add salt and ground spices (onion, ginger, and hot pepper) to
- ✓ Cowpea flour in pieces, beating constantly
- ✓ Add water and stir to create a uniform mixture and a soft dropping.

Cooking

Put oil on fire and add chopped onions to deodorize. Spoonfuls of the mixture should be dropped into the heated oil and fried until golden brown (frying may take about 3 minutes). Remove the cakes from the heated oil, drain them in a strainer, and then place them on paper towels to soak any leftover oil.

Serve hot with porridge.

MAIN DISHES

Fish bra leaves soup.

Ingredients

- 200 g bra leaves
- 300 g groundnut paste
- 50 g fish powder
- 60 g Dawa Dawa
- 15 g hot pepper
- 180 g onion
- 130 g raw groundnuts
- 200 g tomato
- 80 g dry okra
- 10 g bouillon tablet
- Salt
- 3500 ml water

Preparation

- ✓ Remove rotten fish, fish heads, and foreign material or dirt from the lot
- ✓ Pound, the fish
- ✓ Scrape ginger, rinse in clean water, and grind
- ✓ Sort raw groundnut
- ✓ Sort bra leaves, clean, wash with 30 g of the salt water mixture and cut into desirable pieces.
- ✓ Pound Dawa Dawa
- ✓ Grind hot pepper with tomatoes
- ✓ Pound okra
- ✓ Slice onion

Cooking

Groundnut paste should be combined with just enough water for a thin consistency. Stirring regularly, and boil the mixture until oil is released.

Add groundnut paste to a boil kettle, swirl to combine, and then continue to simmer until oil is released.

Add hot pepper and ground tomatoes: pound fish and Dawa Dawa. Allow boiling before adding the crushed bouillon tablet. Okra and uncooked groundnuts should be added. Add one tablespoon of ginger root powder (optional). Salt to taste, then let boil until well cooked. Cut kenaf leaves should be added, stirred, and given some time to boil. Fire extinguished, then served.

Serve with rice balls, banku, or tuo zaafi.

Fish groundnut soup

Ingredients

- 300 g groundnut paste
- 100 g onion
- 30 g fish powder
- 30 g ginger
- 10 g bouillon tablet
- 10 g hot pepper
- 130 g tomato
- 100 g smoked fish
- 3000 ml water
- Salt to taste

Preparation

- ✓ Mix groundnut paste with water and mash
- ✓ Grind tomatoes, hot pepper, ginger, and onion
- ✓ Wash smoked fish, remove waste and bones
- ✓ Break fish into eatable/edible pieces
- ✓ Pound dry fish

Cooking

Stirring occasionally, set the groundnut paste mixture on heat, and boil till oil appears. 2000 ml of water should be added, and the water should cook for 10 to 15 minutes. Please put in the ground veggies and let them boil. Pour the soup in along with the smoked fish that has been ground up and crushed. To taste, add salt. Boil the soup for the desired cooking time.
Serve with kenkey, eba, fufu, banku, tuo zaafi, and (pounded yam, cocoyam, cassava, or plantain)

Shito

Ingredients

- 300 ml vegetable oil
- 140 g fresh onion
- 50 g dry whole hot pepper
- 40 g ginger
- 50 g fish powder
- 250 g fresh tomatoes
- 10 g bouillon tablet
- 200 ml of water
- Salt to taste

Preparation

- ✓ Pound dry, hot pepper together with fresh ginger
- ✓ Pound dry fish

- ✓ Grind tomatoes and hot pepper
- ✓ Chop onion

Cooking

Heating oil Incorporate chopped tomatoes and onions. Place a cover on it and cook. Salt and bouillon pills should also be added. Cover the pan and continue cooking until all the water has evaporated. Pounded hot pepper should be added, stirred, covered, and cooked. Stir in the fish powder while adding it to prevent scorching. Cook the sauce until it turns a deep brown color.

Serve after turning off the heat.

Fish okra soup(Dry)

Ingredients

- 80 g dry okra
- 50 g Dawa Dawa
- One bouillon tablet
- 50 g powdered fish
- Dry onion leaves
- 60 g fresh tomato
- 120 g fresh onion
- 15 g fresh hot pepper
- 1500 ml of water
- Salt to taste

Preparation

- ✓ Boil water
- ✓ Slice onions
- ✓ Pound dry onion leaves (Gabo)
- ✓ Pound fish
- ✓ Grind tomatoes and hot pepper
- ✓ Pound dry okra

Cooking

Light a fire to boil some water. Dawadawa that has been hammered should be included. Allow boiling after adding the fish powder and bouillon tablet. Add ground vegetables and onion slices. Boil the water after adding it. To prevent lumps from forming, sprinkle in little amounts of the dried okra that has been crushed. Add the chopped, dried onion leaves. After a brief period of boiling, turn off the heat.

Serve!

Fish okra soup(Fresh)

Ingredients

- 120 g okra
- 100 g onion
- 30 g powdered fish
- 50 g smoked fish
- 100 ml palm oil
- 15 g fresh hot pepper
- 10 g of bouillon tablet
- 5 g saltpeter
- 500 ml of water
- Salt to taste

Preparation

- ✓ Wash and cut okra into pieces
- ✓ Pound okra with saltpeter in a mortar or beat in a bowl with a
- ✓ kitchen spoon until slimy
- ✓ Wash fish, remove bones, and waste and break into pieces
- ✓ Chop onions
- ✓ Grind tomatoes and hot pepper
- ✓ Pound dry fish

Cooking

Put oil on the fire. In the oil, including the chopped onions, and let them cook, including chopped vegetables. Add fish powder. Add water and the bouillon tablet. Cover it with a lid on it and let it boil. To taste, add salt. Include beaten or crushed okra. After a brief period of boiling, turn off the heat.

Serve with banku, kenkey, or tuo zaafi.

Fish baobab (dry) leaves soup.

Ingredients

- 75 g dry baobab leaves powder
- 50 g Dawa Dawa
- 50 g fish powder
- 10 g bouillon tablet
- 120 g fresh onion
- 160 g fresh tomato
- 50 g tomato paste
- 100 ml palm oil
- 15 g fresh hot pepper
- 500 ml of water
- Salt to taste

Preparation

- ✓ Grind tomato, onion, and hot pepper.
- ✓ Chop onion
- ✓ Pound dry fish
- ✓ Pound Dawa Dawa

Cooking

Set palm oil on fire and let it heat up. When the oil is heated, add the chopped onions and sauté them until they are cooked, including chopped vegetables. Add water and the bouillon pill. Permit to boil. Add salt and fish powder. Stir in the water, cover the pan, and bring to a boil. Sporadically sprinkle kuuka powder made from baobab leaves to prevent lumps from forming.
Boil the food while covered until done.

Fish okra stew

Ingredients

- 220 g okra
- 200 g garden eggs
- 50 g palm oil
- 75 g smoked fish
- 30 g fish powder
- 150 g onion
- 130 g fresh tomato
- 15 g fresh hot pepper
- 10 g bouillon tablet
- 10 g ginger

- 500 ml of water
- Salt to taste

Preparation

- ✓ Wash and cut garden eggs and okra into pieces
- ✓ Wash fish, remove bones and waste, and break them into pieces
- ✓ Chop onions
- ✓ Grind tomatoes, hot pepper, onions, and ginger

Cooking

Heat oil by igniting it. To cook, add chopped onions. Includes diced vegetables And a bouillon pill, water, and smoked salmon.
Set a lid on it and let it boil.
Sprinkle with salt to taste, and mix in the chopped garden eggs. When garden eggs are almost done, add the chopped okra and stir. Cook the chopped onions after adding them. Take out of the fire, then serve.

Fish jute mallow leaves soup.

Ingredients

- 300 g jute mallow leaves
- 50 g Dawa Dawa
- 150 g fresh tomato
- 15 g fresh hot pepper
- 100 g onion
- 50 g fish powder
- 10 g bouillon tablet
- Saltpeter
- 1000 ml water
- Salt to taste

Preparation

- ✓ Wash jute mallow with 30 g added salt water
- ✓ pound jute mallow
- ✓ Grind hot pepper and tomatoes
- ✓ Chop onion into pieces
- ✓ Pound Dawa Dawa
- ✓ Pound dry fish

Cooking

Light a fire to boil some water. Then stir in the Dawa Dawa that has been pounded. Add hot pepper and ground tomatoes. Allow boiling after adding chopped onion and spicy pepper powder. Steam the jute mallow in a different saucepan with a bit of water. Add saltpeter and steam for 5 to 10 minutes to make it slimy. Stir in the heated jute mallow. To taste, add salt. If the mixture is too stout, add water and let it boil. When cooked, serve.

Serve with banku, kenkey, and tuo zaafi.

Amaranth leaves stew

Ingredients
- 550 g amaranth leaves
- 430 g tomatoes
- 10 g bouillon tablet
- 15 g ginger
- 10 g garlic
- 200 g onion
- 70 g tomato paste
- 15 g hot pepper
- 50 g fish powder
- 250 g agushi (melon seed)
- 2700 ml water

- Salt to taste

Preparation

- ✓ Sort aleefu leaves, clean them, and wash them with 30 g of salt water
- ✓ Cut leaves into pieces and blanch
- ✓ Wash and grind hot pepper and tomatoes
- ✓ Scrape ginger, rinse in clean water, and grind
- ✓ Slice onion
- ✓ Grind the agushi into a soft paste
- ✓

Cooking

Heat palm oil by setting a fire. Fry the onion after introducing it. Add hot pepper and ground tomatoes. Stir in the tomato paste and carry to a boil. Stir, close the lid, and simmer. Salt to taste and add the bouillon tablet. Agushi should be added, cooked in lumps, and without stirring. After lumps develop, stir to combine evenly. Amaranth leaves that have been blanched should be added. Stir and boil for a few minutes. Fire extinguished, then served.

Serve with boiling yam, banku, kenkey, or simple white rice.

CHAPTER-3

SOME AUTHENTIC GHANAIAN RECIPES

Spinach Stew

Serves 6

Ingredient

- Two boxes of spinach
- Four medium tomatoes
- 6 oz smoked fish
- 10 oz egushi
- 1 cup olive oil
- 1 tbsp pepper
- One large onion
- 4 oz Kobi
- 1 Maggi cube

Directions

Separate the smoked fish (or turkey) into medium-sized pieces. Drain after 30 minutes of cooking. Place aside. Thaw the spinach and drain the liquid.
The sliced onion should be added to a medium saucepan with pepper, Kobi, and olive oil. Cook for 4 minutes on medium heat. Add tomato slices to the onion mixture. Maggie cube is added; cook for 15 to 20 minutes. Make the stew with smoked fish (or turkey). For 5-8 minutes, let simmer. Combine tomato with egushi (ground melon seeds) and 1/2 cup of water. Include drained spinach and 3/4 cup fish stock, and boil for 6 minutes. Simmer for a further 4 minutes. Cut the heat and let it cool.

Served with ampesie or rice.

Beef Stew

Serves 8

Ingredients

- 2 lb stewing beef
- 1/4 cup olive oil
- 4 tbsp tomato paste
- 3 tsp fresh
- One garlic clove

- 1 tsp salt
- Four medium onions
- 2.5 tsp red pepper

Directions

In a medium heating pan, brown the beef for 10 minutes while adding sliced onions, minced garlic, and salt. Remove the meat and bake it at 350° for 20 minutes or until tender. Add onions and olive oil to the medium frying pan that housed the beef. Cook for 10 minutes with oil.

Combine pepper and tomatoes. Put it with the parsley in a medium saucepan. Please take out the roasted meat and add it to the tomato sauce. Allow the beef sauce to boil for 10 minutes on low heat. After 4 minutes of simmering, remove from heat and let cool.

Serve with Wake, Campsie, and cooked brown rice.

Palm-nut Soup

Serves 6

Ingredients

- One can palm nut
- 1 lb chicken breast
- Two medium onions,
- Three medium tomatoes
- 1/2 tin tomato paste
- One medium fish
- 8 oz mushrooms
- Three blue crabs
- crab

- One medium jalapeño

Directions

Trim meat to stewing size after washing. In a medium saucepan, combine the beef, tomato paste, one chopped onion, and optional salt. Cook for 9-10 mins, stirring occasionally, or until the onions are tender.

In a separate pan, cook fresh tomatoes, peppers, and onions for 10 minutes. Clean your fish, crabs, and mushrooms. Cut crabs into bits and divide fish in two. Add to the meat that is cooking.

Combine onions and tomatoes. Add mixture and 1/3 pint of water to the meat up to boil. Include palm nuts in the meat mixture; add water.

Continue blending the soup. Cook the soup for 25 minutes or until red oil begins to secrete on top. Decrease to 5 minutes on low heat.

Enjoy!

New Waakye Recipe

Serves 6

Ingredient

- 1 cup of rice
- 3 cups black-eyed
- 1/3 tsp baking soda
- One can of coconut milk
- beans
- 1/2 tsp salt
- 6 cups of water

Directions

Clean black-eyed beans, then add them to a medium pot. Cook on high heat for about 20 minutes with a cover of 3/4 full of water. After a quick boil, lower the heat to medium to simmer.

Add approximately 2 cups of water for 10 minutes
if the black-eyed peas are not soft.
Add the rice and coconut milk when the black-eyed peas have finished cooking; add 1.5 cups or so of water. Stir with baking soda and salt, then simmer for 20 minutes. Stir with a serving fork, lower the heat, and simmer for 10 minutes.
By this time, the rice and beans' color will have changed to a pale shade.

Please turn off the stove and keep it cool. Accompany beef, goat, fish, or chicken stew with different dishes.

Serve!

Peanut Butter Soup

Serves 6

Ingredients

- One can make palm nut
- 1 lb chicken breast
- One whole fish
- 8 oz mushrooms
- One large onion
- Three medium tomatoes
- 1/2 tin tomato paste
- Two medium crabs
- 1/2 lb peanut butter
- Two medium jalapeños

Directions

Trim meat to stewing size after cleaning. In a large saucepan, cook the beef, tomato paste, and chopped onions for 8 to 10 minutes or until the meat is cooked.

In a separate pan, cook the tomatoes, peppers, and onions for about 10 minutes. Clean your fish, crabs, and mushrooms. Cut into fragments. Combine onions and tomatoes. Place 1/4 pint of the mixture over the meat. It is heating to a boil. In a blender, combine 1/4 pint of water and peanut butter. Pour over in a pot until smooth and golden brown over medium heat.

Cook the soup for 20 minutes after adding the peanut butter mixture, stirring often.

The meat should be tender, and the water in the soup shouldn't be separated from it.

Chicken Stew

Serves 6

Ingredients

- 2 lb chicken
- 1/4 cup olive oil
- Four large tomatoes
- 4 tbsp tomato paste
- 3 tsp dried parsley
- Two medium onions
- One small onion
- Four basil leaves, chopped
- One large garlic clove, chopped
- One jalapeño

Directions

First, wash and season the chicken. Add onions, garlic, 2 1/2 tsp. Salt and 1/2 tsp. Pepper powder. The oven to 250 degrees.
Sauté beef for 10 minutes in a medium saucepan; remove and bake the chicken at 250 degrees until it is brown. In a saucepan, cook onions in Cooking (olive) oil for five minutes. Combine tomatoes and jalapenos in a blender. Onto the onion mixture, pour.

Add salt, basil, parsley, and any other seasonings you choose. Include tomato paste. Cook for 20-22 min on low heat, stirring periodically until a layer of crimson oil forms on the top. Add chicken and stock to the tomato stew.

Ten minutes of intense heat simmering. Adjust seasoning as necessary, then boil for 4 minutes.

Pair with amnesia, kenkey, or cooked brown rice.

Enjoy!

Grilled Tilapia

Serves 2

Ingredients

- 2 tilapia or mackerel
- One large onion
- Three pieces of garlic
- 1/4 tsp salt
- 2 oz fresh ginger
- One large jalapeno pepper
- 1 tbsp olive oil

Directions

Split or triangle the fish. After cleaning:
1. Please put them in a bowl.
2. Combine olive oil, jalapenos, onions, garlic, and ginger.
3. Pour over the fish.
4. For 15 to 20 minutes, allow marinating.

Set oven temperature to 380 degrees. Broil for 8 minutes on each side on low heat. Cook fish for another 5 minutes on each side. Add fresh red, yellow, and onion peppers as garnish and fried yams, kenkey, or banku. Or, serve the vegetables by themselves.

Enjoy!

Meat Pie

Serves 8

Ingredients

- 2 cups white flour
- 1 cup wheat flour
- Two tomatoes
- 2 tbsp olive oil
- 1 cup carrots
- 1/4 cup peas
- Three sticks of butter
- 1/2 lb lean beef
- One large onion

- 1/8 cup evaporated milk
- Two large bay leaves
- 1 tsp thyme

Directions

Filled with Meat

Add 1/2 teaspoon of black or white pepper to the meat. Cook till very dark gray or brown. Keep away from the heat and place in a bowl for later. In a large frying pan, sauté chopped onions with two tablespoons of oil, stirring at medium heat.
After stirring for three minutes, add the diced tomatoes. Add the carrots, peas, bay leaf, and thyme and simmer for 5 minutes.
Return the meat to the mixture—three more minutes of cooking. Remove the bay leaf, turn off the heat, and cool the mixture.

Pie Crust

Set oven temperature to 380 degrees. Coat a baking sheet with baking oil. It is covered with flour; lay it aside. Mix the flour and margarine sticks for 8 minutes in a mixing basin.
To make the pastry, evenly distribute 1/8 cup of water over the ingredients. Mix slowly. The pie shouldn't cling to the spoon and should drop off quickly. Shape the dough into a ball the size of your fist. Roll the pastry balls on a floured cutting board or work surface on a spotless surface.

Lightly brush the area with a baking brush or your fingertips after dipping them in water. Place beef sauce in the center of the pastry. Roll the plain pastry to cover the exposed portion and seal it by raising the other side.

Use a fork dusted with flour to push the packed pastry closed. Place in a line on a baking sheet. For a golden brown, lightly brush with evaporated milk.
Bake for 30 minutes at 350 degrees. Check the middle with a skewer.

The stick is prepared. Enjoy!

Salmon Soup

Serves 4

Ingredients

- 2 lbs salmon
- 2 oz fresh ginger
- One large onion
- Three medium tomatoes
- One large jalapeno pepper
- 1/4 tsp salt

Directions

Clean the fish, then chop it into six pieces. Add salt and pepper to taste. Place aside. For 10 minutes, cook tomatoes, pepper, ginger, and onions in a pan. Remove the mixture and purée it. Add the pureed sauce and around 1/3 pint of water to a pot. Prepare for about 20 minutes. Include the seasoned salmon. Prepare for approximately 15 minutes on medium.

Remove from heat, then serve.

Rice Balls

Serves 6

Ingredients

- 3 cups Carolina or
- Jasmin rice
- 7 cups of water

Directions

Place the rice and 4 cups of water in a 10" saucepan.

Cover and heat until boiling. Keep the heat low to medium and simmer for 20 minutes.

Remove the cover from the pan and lightly fluff with a serving fork. After adding the second cup of water, let the rice simmer for 10 minutes.

Open the rice and examine the consistency. It ought to be more tender than typical rice.

Cooking and adding water as necessary should continue. Avoid the heat and mash with a wooden stick or potato masher. Roll rice into golf balls using wet hands after scooping it with an ice cream scooper like a ball size. Continue to form balls out of all the rice.

Serve with a side of black-eyed beans, peanut butter soup, or palm nut soup.

Koose Black eyed-bean fritters

Serves 4

Ingredients

- 1/4 cup wheat flour
- 3/4 bag of black-eyed beans
- 1-inch ginger
- One large onion
- 1/4 cup olive oil
- 1/4 tsp. baking powder
- 1/4 tsp. pepper
- 1/4 tsp salt

Directions

Black-eyed beans should be soaked in water overnight. Under running water, wash the beans and drain them. Set the oven to 370°F. Remove loose skins and combine the pepper, onions, and celery in a food processor.
Include salt, pepper, ginger, and onions. Blend until the mixture is relatively smooth. Use proper seasoning. Add the baking powder and wheat flour to bind the mixture. Add salt, pepper, ginger, and onions. Move the mixture to a prepared baking pan. Place the glass dish in the oven and cook for 30 to 40 minutes. Remove and set on a cooling rack.

Divide into portions and serve.

Baked Plantains

Serves 4

Ingredients

- ✓ Six full Ripe Plantains

Directions

Set the oven to 380°F. Peel plantains and slices each into four pieces. Set a baking rack underneath them.

Bake in the oven for 28-30 minutes or until golden brown.

Pure Jollof Rice

Serves 6

Ingredient

- 3 cups rice
- 1/4 cup olive oil
- 1/2 tin tomato paste
- 2 tsp fresh parsley
- 2 tsp fresh basil
- Two dried bay leaves
- 1/2 tbsp salt
- 1 lb chicken breast
- Two large tomatoes
- One large onion
- Two jalapeno peppers
- Four cloves garlic
- One box low salt beef
- broth
- 1/2 lb fresh green beans

Directions

Brown the meat, drain the stock, and save both for another time. If you're using fresh jalapenos, mix them with fresh tomatoes and onions before adding them to the pan. Or Put the sliced or sauté pepper and chopped onions in a skillet for about five minutes.

Include tomato paste, basil, minced garlic, tomato slices or dice, and bay leaves—salt, leaves, and whatever spices you choose.
When the sauce becomes more subdued, continue simmering for 10 to 15 minutes.

Include a few pieces of the sauce meat or dried herrings. Add the stock to a quick boil, then stir in the rice.

Keep the heat low and cook for approximately 10 minutes. Add the green beans afterward, and whisk or mash with a fork. Give it five minutes or so to steam.

Turn off the heat and serve the meat that has been sautéed separately.

Light Soup

Serves 4

Ingredients

- 1 lb beef
- One whole fish
- Three medium tomatoes
- 1/2 tin tomato paste
- One large jalapeno pepper
- 8 oz mushrooms
- Two medium crabs

- One large onion
- 1/4 tsp salt
- 3 cups water

Directions

Trim meat to stewing size after cleaning. Mix the beef, salt, tomato paste, and chopped onion in a skillet on medium heat—steam for roughly 6 minutes with a cover.

In another pan, sauté tomatoes, onions, and fresh pepper until soft. Drain and purée the onion mixture.

Add three cups of water, and then boil for 15 minutes. Take out the tomatoes, fresh peppers, and onions. Mash into a purée. Add the pureed sauce to the Soup. To the broth, add meat. Split the fish in half after cleaning.

Carry to a boil and cook for 12-15 minutes.

Bofrot

Serves 4

Ingredients

- 1.5 cups flour
- 1.5 tsp active yeast
- One egg
- 1/4 tsp salt
- 1/2 tsp grated nutmeg
- 1/4 cup sugar
- 1 cup water
- 1/8 cup warm water

- 1/4 tsp vegetable oil
- Two kebab sticks

Directions

Fill a mixing bowl with warm water. Add the yeast and a dash of salt, then let it rise until foam develops on the top. Combine the egg, sugar, salt, flour, and nutmeg. For about 5 minutes, thoroughly blend.

Let the mixture stand for 2-3 hours until it doubles in volume. Put the vegetable oil in a medium pot and let it heat for approximately 8 minutes on a medium-heat burner.

Scoop a little amount of the dough mixture with your hands or a tablespoon. Pour fragments into the hot oil. To turn, use the kebab stick. Remove with a flat spatula after frying for 3 minutes or until golden brown.

It may be garnished with powdered sugar or served with honey.

CHAPTER -4

RECIPES INFORMATION

In The Cookbook, Which Included:

- ➢ Breakfast
- ➢ One-Pot Dishes
- ➢ Accompaniments –
- ➢ Main Dishes (Soups and Stews)
- ➢ Drinks
- ➢ Snacks
- ➢ Healthy Recipes

CONCLUSION

Ghanaian cuisine is diverse and flavorful, reflecting the country's history and culture. Various spices, herbs, vegetables, and a wide range of meats and seafood characterize it.

Staple Foods:

Ghana's leading staple food is fufu, made from cassava, plantains, or yams. It is usually served with a soup or stew made from vegetables, meat, or fish. Other staple foods include banku, kenkey, and tuo zaafi.

Soups and Stews:

Ghanaian cuisine is known for its flavorful soups and stews. One famous soup is groundnut soup, which is made with ground peanuts, vegetables, and meat or fish. Another famous stew is palm nut soup with palm nuts, vegetables, and meat or fish.

Meats:

Meat is an integral part of Ghanaian cuisine. Beef, chicken, and goat are popular meats, as are fish and seafood. Meat is often grilled, stewed, or fried and is usually seasoned with various spices and herbs.

Spices and Herbs:

The use of a wide range of spices and herbs characterizes Ghanaian cuisine. The most commonly used spices include ginger, garlic, cumin, coriander, and chili peppers. Popular herbs include basil, thyme, and parsley.

Vegetables:

Vegetables are essential to Ghanaian cuisine, and many different types are used. The most commonly used vegetables include tomatoes, onions, eggplants, and okra.

Snacks:

Ghanaian cuisine has a variety of delicious snacks, including the chin, a sweet, crunchy snack made from flour, sugar, and spices. Another popular snack is kelewele, which is made from ripe plantains that have been seasoned with herbs and fried until crispy.

Beverages:

Ghanaian cuisine has a variety of delicious beverages, including palm wine, which is made from the sap of palm trees. Another popular beverage is sobolo, a sweet, tangy drink from hibiscus flowers. Ghana is also known for its delicious coffee grown in its fertile highlands.

Dining Etiquette:

In Ghana, dining is often a communal experience with family-style meals. Eating with your right hand and using your left hand to hold a drinking cup is customary. When dining with others, waiting for everyone to be served before beginning to eat is considered polite.

Like most developing nations in Sub-Saharan Africa, Ghana is undergoing an economical and nutritional transition marked by increased obesity and obesity-related illnesses among adults, particularly urban dwellers, including cardiovascular disease, Type 2 diabetes mellitus, hypertension, and some forms of cancer. This might be due to various things, such as globalization, migration, and the flood of low-cost foods that are nutrient-poor and high in calories.

The rise of various international fast-food franchises, which are increasingly becoming a frequent sight in Accra and other major towns like Kumasi and Takoradi, is noteworthy among elements associated with globalization. As a result, traditional Ghanaian meals are gradually replaced with nutrient-poor, high-energy foods.

In Ghana, dietitians are crucial in designing and implementing successful nutrition education initiatives that slow the spread of non-communicable illnesses. Four universities now teach dietitians at the undergraduate and graduate levels, with the University of Ghana beginning the process in 2004. More than 150 qualified dietitians work in both the public and commercial sectors, promoting healthy eating with an emphasis on selecting foods that are readily accessible locally and educating consumers about better ways to prepare food.

Book Information

We are delighted to be capable of getting out a Ghanaian cookbook. We have tried to be more careful in revising the book and believe it will help every level chef who starts their life in cooking. If they benefit from the book, our labor will be worthwhile. We also welcome good comments and suggestions for further improvement of it. Thanks for choosing us.

Suggestions

❖ Avoid haram ingredients

THE END

Printed in Great Britain
by Amazon